A SMALL HISTORY OF VIRTUE

ALWAYS DO WHAT'S GOOD

SANDRA L. DINELLO

Always Do What's Good

Copyright © 2025 by Sandra L. DiNello

All rights reserved. No part of this book may be reproduced or used in any manner without written permission of the copyright owner except for the use of quotations in a book review.

Book Cover Design and Interior Formatting by 100 Covers.

ISBN: 979-8-9937567-1-4 (paperback)

ISBN: 979-8-9937567-0-7 (ebook)

*For my mother, Sandra L. DiNello
whose words have been waiting quietly since 1997—
and whose heart for truth and virtue never faded.*

With joy, I offer these pages to honor your work and your words.

"I believe in the sun even when it is not shining.
I believe in love even when I cannot feel it.
I believe in God even when He is silent."

— Inscription from a WWII concentration camp
Bastille prison wall

CONTENTS

Foreword ix

Author's Note xi

What is "Good"? 1

Lillian Trasher 7

Drana Bojaxhiu 11

Abdul Aziz Ibn Saud 15

Prince Salman 19

Bill Havens 23

Sara Ann Roosevelt 27

Queen Victoria 31

William Wilberforce 35

Rosa Parks 39

Corrie Ten Boom 43

George Washington Carver 47

Mohandas Gandhi 51

President Abraham Lincoln 53

The Cosmos and the Cross 55

About the Author...61

Kristen Miller's Biography 63

FOREWORD

by Kristen Miller

There are few voices in this world that carry both wisdom and warmth — the kind of voice that not only teaches but touches the soul. The author of this treasured collection, my dear mentor and friend, is one of those voices. A former English teacher with a passport full of stamps and a heart full of stories, she has lived a life rich in culture, learning, and love. Her stories — whether told in person or written on the page — have a way of staying with you long after the last word is spoken.

Always Do What's Good is a beautiful extension of her life's message. In these pages, you'll find true stories drawn from history, thoughtfully retold to awaken something noble within us — courage, kindness, integrity, and hope. These aren't fairy tales, but real accounts of people who chose goodness, often when it was costly, inconvenient, or even dangerous. The result is a tapestry of human virtue, stitched across times and cultures, reminding us that goodness is always relevant, always possible, and always worth it.

What I love most about this book is how effortlessly it invites us to reflect. Each story — short, compelling, and full of heart — leaves you with something to ponder and a quiet challenge to become a better human. You'll turn the last page feeling inspired to lean into kindness, choose courage over comfort, and live with more intention than you did before.

This is the kind of book you'll want to keep on the shelf and pull out often — for a dose of courage, a reminder of kindness, or just a good story to share.

It is a great honor to write this foreword. The woman behind these stories has not been my teacher in a classroom, but in something far greater — life. She has taught me lessons no textbook could offer, given advice that could outdo any therapist, and offered counsel so wise it would put the best of counselors to shame. Her wisdom is unmatched. She's taught me how to listen well, live fully, and lead with heart. And now, through this book, she gets to pass on those same lessons to you.

May these pages remind you, as they have reminded me, that no matter where you are or what era you live in — it is always right to do what is good.

Warmly,

Kristen Miller

AUTHOR'S NOTE

This book is a collection of true stories drawn from history, retold here to inspire readers with examples of virtue lived out across times and cultures. Every figure mentioned in these pages is a real person, and the central events described are based on either actual historical records or long-standing traditions about their lives.

In some cases, the exact details of conversations, actions, or settings have been adapted, condensed, or written in a way that makes them more accessible to readers, especially younger audiences. Dialogue is not intended to be a verbatim historical record but rather an imaginative retelling consistent with the known character and circumstances of the people involved.

While every effort has been made to honor the truth of these individuals' lives and the virtues they embodied, it is also important to remember that no person — even those who have done great good — is without fault. Some of the people featured in these stories, such as Mohandas Gandhi, held beliefs or made choices that were wrong and even harmful, despite their remarkable courage and example in other areas. Their stories remind us that virtue and failure often exist side by side in the same life, and that we can both admire the good they did and learn from their mistakes.

This book is meant to highlight timeless truths and to spark reflection on the universal value of virtue in all times and places.

— Sandra L. DiNello

WHAT IS "GOOD"?

The ancient Greeks and Romans considered prudence, justice, courage, and temperance to be of such importance that they called them "cardinal" virtues. This meant that they were the basis upon which all other virtues must be built.

As the Western world became Christianized, the biblical virtues of faith, hope, and love were included with the cardinal virtues as the foundation stones of society's value system.

What exactly is virtue, that such importance has been placed upon it? It is defined, at least in part, as moral excellence, right action and right thinking, and goodness of character. Virtue, then, is not something we can hold, but it is an intangible nobility that can touch and lift our lives.

Virtue in that sense is rather like the wind: We can't catch it or put it in a bottle. We can't see it or own it, but we can see its effect, everywhere that it is present!

It's sometimes difficult today to see the evidence of virtue in our lives. Perhaps this is because we're reluctant to say, "This is good," for if we identify something as good, the reverse of it must be "bad." We try very hard not to be judgmental because the one thing our modern world does not value is the discernment to say something is wrong!

This little book dares to step forward and say that some things indeed are good, are virtuous. They deserve to be respected by all of us, not because I say they're good or you say they're good, but because in all times, in all places—as near as our own neighborhoods (around the corner) and as far off as the most distantly removed culture (around the world) —all people have agreed that these things are virtuous.

With that stamp of approval upon them, it is important that we embrace these virtues, soak them into ourselves like water into a sponge, and that we assume the responsibility for passing them along.

We may assent to (agree with) the idea of virtue. Our common sense may tell us that life will improve if we live unselfishly, kindly, politely, and if others around us do the same. Our common sense and our ability to observe our own actual behavior and the behavior of others reveals to us that unselfishness, kindness, and courtesy are not always in evidence, especially when they are most needed! When we feel angry or threatened or cheated, for example, it is unlikely that we will evidence these traits that we claim to admire. We ask ourselves if there is some foundation upon which we can build these traits that will hold up even when we are under the kind of pressure that these negative feelings stir up within us. The good news is that there is!

If we can accept the idea that there is something greater than our own immediate desires, something loftier than ourselves to which we may lift our hope, then we can be motivated to do the right and honorable thing, to believe in the best, even when to do so flies in the face of logic.

That concept of something apart from and above ourselves was beautifully expressed by one whose name is unknown. He was a prisoner in the Bastille, a notorious prison in France during the horrible days of the French Revolution. He had no writing implements as he awaited the day of his execution, but he managed to scratch into the stone wall of his cell this beautiful affirmation of the virtue of faith in God. He said, "I believe in the sun, even when it is not shining. I believe in love, even when I can't feel it. I believe in God, even when He is silent.".

If we cultivate within ourselves that kind of unshakable faith in God, we will not soon be selfish, unkind, discourteous to others; we will not soon allow ourselves to be ensnared by the allure of some of the negative things that pervade our society—things like drugs, substance abuse of any kind, promiscuity, or lack of self-esteem. We will be empowered by faith in God's love for us to stand against temptation in any form. We will also be empowered to build upon that foundation of faith; we will be empowered to build virtue into our lives!

The vignettes that follow evidence a wide range of virtues in the lives of famous people. We would be advantaged as individuals and as a nation if we would resolve to follow their examples.

LILLIAN TRASHER

In the early part of the twentieth century; a young missionary went to the country of Egypt. What was most unusual about the missionary was the fact that she was a woman. Many Muslim lands do not easily accept the idea of a woman being alone. They believe all women need to be under the protection of the men in their families. A woman without a man as her protector is considered not only a great curiosity, but is also an object of scorn.

This courageous young missionary, Lillian Trasher, endured the persecution that went along with being a lone woman in a hostile environment without retaliating in any way against those who made her life difficult. She simply went about her God-appointed task of loving and helping the many poor people around her. Her efforts were strongest on behalf of orphaned children who, because they had no home and no one to care for them, had the hard life of living in the streets. Miss Trasher took in many of these homeless children and nurtured them physically, academically, and spiritually.

Before long, she had established a large orphanage that housed and helped hundreds of poor Egyptian children. The people who had scorned her began to look upon her as a loving, godly woman who was truly a friend to the people of Egypt!

When Lillian Trasher died, the government of Egypt did something it had never done before for any woman. The Egyptian flag was lowered to half-staff, and a national day of mourning was declared to honor the great gift of kindness she had given. The orphanage that she established long ago is still there today, helping needy children to be educated, nurtured, and loved.

Lillian Trasher's sacrificial life has gone virtually unnoticed outside of Egypt and outside of her own denomination, but the love of Jesus within her heart that motivated her to serve the lowly and the helpless of the world has stirred within other hearts as well.

DRANA BOJAXHIU

In the early twentieth century, in the land of Macedonia, a young mother cared for her three children. The woman's name was Dranafile (Drana) Bojaxhiu. She worked hard, as most people did in those days before modern technology gave us so many conveniences for our daily tasks.

Drana and her husband both tried to make life good for their children, and, indeed, they enjoyed a measure of prosperity. Her husband's untimely death, however, ended this prosperity for Drana and her children. Although the circumstances of his passing were suspicious, Drana refused to allow herself or her children to harbor bitterness or hatred. Her philosophy was that she and her family could "do without money, but can't do with sin." She resolved that she would not "allow any impurity" into her heart. Her children embraced her determination to face their circumstances with joy and praise to God instead of with despair and bitterness.

Drana's daughter Agnes seemed most profoundly affected by her mother's complete faith in God and His goodness. It caused her to pursue a direction in her life that few women in that day chose. Instead of desiring simply to marry and raise a family, she decided to become a teacher. She left her home in Macedonian to attend a school in the faraway country of Ireland that was called the Loreto Abbey. There she mastered English so she could realize her dream of teaching the poor children of India, which was then an English colony. Even though attaining her goal had many barriers, Agnes never forgot her mother's words, "Put your hand in God's, and walk all the way with Him."

In 1928, at the age of eighteen, Agnes Bojaxhiu set sail for India and a lifetime of service to the poor. Her faith and her love, like her mother Drana's, ran deep and sure. In the life of Agnes Bojaxhiu, we saw the beautiful fruition of the promise of the Bible, "As a mother is before her daughter, so shall her daughter be" (Ezek. 16:44). Drana's life of commitment to faith in God and purity of thought, word, and deed, and service to others have been evidenced before the eyes of the world through the life of her daughter Agnes, who we know as Mother Theresa.

ABDUL AZIZ IBN SAUD

As it is the responsibility of parents to "bring up their children in the wisdom and instruction of the Lord" (Eph. 6:4, ESV), it is the God-ordained duty of children to honor their parents. In our modern world, many have lost that sense of respect for their parents, that deference that was once the mark of esteem upon every parent/child relationship.

One of the most beautiful stories ever told of the love and respect of a young man for his father comes from the land of Saudi Arabia. The first king of that vast desert realm was a man named Abdul Aziz Ibn Saud. King Abdul Aziz had unified the many desert tribes of the Arabian Peninsula through his bravery and his diplomacy. He was a wise individual who recognized that not only power made a man or a nation great, but also virtue. He was recognized for his fairness and integrity in all his dealings. The king enjoyed the loyalty of his subjects, and he had many slaves to do his bidding. However, in the matter of caring for his elderly father, he did not merely assign a slave to see to the old man's needs. He himself though he were the king, viewed it as his responsibility to assist his father.

One day, it is told, the feeble old gentleman was having difficulty mounting his camel. In his youth, he had effortlessly climbed aboard the large beast. When the constraints of old age rendered him unable to achieve his goal independently, his son, the great king, got down on his hands and knees and allowed his father to step upon his back so that he could mount his camel!

A man with the authority to command not only any slave, but also any soldier or any subject to perform that task for his father, chose instead to do it himself—not because the others wouldn't have been willing, not because the others wouldn't have been capable had the king not humbled himself on his father's behalf! King Abdul Aziz submitted himself to be his father's footstool because he so deeply respected the man who had raised him!

We today would do well to emulate this great monarch. Honoring parents is something we don't see as often as we should in our modern world, but the biblical admonition to "honor your father and mother" was not limited to Saudi Arabia or to the people of Abdul Aziz's generation. It is true for all people in all times. If King Abdul Aziz could lay his body down as a step stool for his father, so should we honor our parents by the extension of our love and kindness and our respect to them.

PRINCE SALMAN

Because of the example established by King Abdul Aziz within his family, his children grew up to respect their parents and in turn taught their children the value of this virtue. The king's descendants are among the wealthiest people in the world, but in spite of the privilege their great revenues afford them, they still maintain the virtue demonstrated by their grandfather.

In the spring of 1984, a young Saudi Arabian prince paid an unusual visit to his mother at the behest of his father, Prince Salman, governor of the capital city of Riyadh. The young man, Sultan bin Salman Al Saud, had an opportunity to embark upon a wonderful adventure, one that few people in the history of the world had ever shared. Before making his plans, Prince

Sultan did what any well-brought-up Middle Easterner would have done: He extended the respect to his father by asking his permission to finalize his plans.

His father was delighted at the prospect, but qualified his permission. Prince Sultan must first obtain the permission of two others, his Uncle Fahd, the reigning king of Saudi Arabia, and his mother. King Fahd, like Prince Salman, was pleased and eagerly granted his permission to the young prince's request. When he went to his mother, however, she resisted, as any loving mother would have done under the circumstances. Although her son was a grown man, an accomplished officer in the Saudi Royal Air Force, and an experienced pilot, she was reluctant to sanction the adventure he was planning.

Prince Sultan was not easily dissuaded from his mission of persuasion, however. He assured his mother of the safety of his mission, of his complete preparedness for carrying out his responsibilities to a safe conclusion. He reminded her of what an honor it would be to be a participant in this grand journey, and, we can imagine, plied her with his charms, as sons have ever done to win their requests from their doting mothers! After many days of persuasion, his mother laid aside her fears and granted her son the permission he sought of her.

Having secured the permission of his father and those his father required, Prince Sultan returned to the United States, where he had been in training in the aerospace program. That spring, he became the first man from his nation, the first man of the Muslim faith, and the first member of the Saudi royal family to travel in space as an astronaut!

The heartwarming tales of King Abdul Aziz and his grandson, Prince Sultan bin Salman Al Saud, are clear evidence of the impact that parental example has upon the children of a family. It is at the knee of their parents that children learn many of the virtues for which society longs. Parents cannot convey values to their children if they do not practice them themselves. We are not likely to find children who respect their parents if they have not seen respect modeled for them by their parents. It is important that parents value one another and value the treasure that their children are.

BILL HAVENS

Ideally, a child is loved and wanted by both parents, and both parents let their child see what a precious gift they consider each child to be. When parents show love and respect to their children—make them important—it is easier for a child to respect them in return. A beautiful story of a father's love and respect for his wife and his unborn child occurred many years ago, in 1924. The man's name was Bill Havens, and he was an expert canoeist who had been picked to represent the United States at the Olympic Games that were being held that year in Paris, France. When Mr. Havens realized that his child was due to be born at the same time the Olympics were scheduled, he decided to stay at home with his wife to await the important event. Their son was born, and he always knew how dear he was to his father.

Mr. Havens never lost interest in the Olympics, and followed them quite closely through the years. In 1952, twenty-eight years after he declined to represent his country in this great international event, he received a telegram from another Olympic participant that said, "Thanks for waiting around for me to be born. . . . I'm coming home with the gold medal you should have won. Your loving son, Frank."

Being there for his son cost Mr. Havens his own opportunity for the gold, but his son's achievement brought him great satisfaction, and his son's love and respect brought him far greater and more lasting joy than a gold medal, won at the expense of being present for his son's birth, could have ever done.

Honor encompasses all the other gifts that a child is admonished in scripture to give to his parents, and it is from his parents that he learns what honor is and how it is to be shared within a family.

It is very difficult for a child who has not learned respect and honor for parental authority within his home to grow up to value others of society's authority figures. Teachers are not esteemed, governmental representatives are not held in high regard, if a young person has not been given and expected to give honor in the home. When we have respect within families, the family unit is strengthened. Strong families build strong nations. The Bible says that we must "[grant] honor to whom honor is due," (Rom. 13:7, NRSV) and that includes those such as teachers and governmental officials who are in authority over us, as well as to our parents.

SARA ANN ROOSEVELT

In the 1930s Franklin Delano Roosevelt was elected as president of the United States of America. Mr. Roosevelt had been born into a wealthy family and had been raised very properly according to the correct manners of the day. He was not only a great statesman, but a fine gentleman in an age when courtesy and respect were shown in small ways as well as in large, such as a man tipping his hat to greet a lady or rising from his seat when a lady entered the room.

Soon after he was elected president, Franklin Roosevelt went to visit his mother, Sara Ann Roosevelt, at her home in New York. When he entered the room where his mother was awaiting his arrival, she rose from her chair to greet him. Courtesy did not require an elderly woman to get up to greet a guest. To have remained seated would have been entirely appropriate for Mrs. Roosevelt.

Her son said, "Mother, please don't get up for me!"

She turned to him and said graciously, "I'm not standing for you, Franklin, I'm standing for the president of the United States."

Today, we have allowed our respect for the office of those in authority to be diminished. We rightly guard our right to disagree with officials, but we have lost our ability to disagree agreeably with the individual while regarding his position with esteem. Whether to those in authority in the classroom or in the Oval Office, we need to express the respect Mrs. Roosevelt extended to her son—who just happened to also be her president!

QUEEN VICTORIA

We've already established that it's easier for children to respect parents who model respect before them. So, too, it is easier to respect authority figures who extend respect to those whose position in life may not be so lofty as their own.

Some people seem to attempt to make themselves feel important by putting down someone else. It is as though they attempt to lift themselves up by trampling upon the feelings of others. Some people in leadership positions take that approach, but the truly great ones exude a graciousness that puts everyone around them at ease.

We travel to England for the story of a great lady who lived more than a century ago. She was beautiful and wise, and she was the most powerful person in the world in her day. She was

Queen Victoria, and she ruled over the vast British Empire (1837-1901), upon which the sun never set.

Because of her wealth and authority and power, people deferred to her. They respected her, and her subjects obeyed all her commands. Yet for all the pomp that surrounded her and all the vast power at her command, she maintained a graciousness, which is kindness, and she maintained courtesy and compassion, even to supposed "inferiors." One night, a grand banquet was held at the palace. Many guests had been invited, and one guest who sat at her table was not accustomed to all the niceties of the high society in which he found himself.

At each place setting, a small finger bowl had been placed into which the fingers could be dipped before eating. He thought the water was for drinking, and he picked up his finger bowl and took a sip! The other guests became quite amused at his expense—they felt superior, for their manners at the table were far better than his! His hostess, however, did not want her guest to be embarrassed. To spare him discomfort at his faux pas (his mistake), Queen Victoria picked up her finger bowl and drank from it too!

When the others saw the graciousness of their queen, they realized how unkind they'd been. Soon others at the table followed the lead of their sovereign and drank from their finger bowls as well!

We may not reign over a vast empire as Queen Victoria did, but each of us has the opportunity to be considerate of the feelings of others, to put them at ease when they feel like outsiders. When we step forward to do the right thing, others will follow suit. By reaching out in this manner, we evidence our confidence in ourselves. Like that glorious monarch of old, we show that our self-worth does not depend on belittling others. A truism is that a big person never needs to make others feel small.

WILLIAM WILBERFORCE

The reality is that governments and their representatives do not always comport themselves in ways that are worthy of our emulation. Sometimes, official government policy is such that it requires men of conscience to stand up in protest against it. William Wilberforce was such a man. He certainly was an unlikely hero. The movies have successfully convinced most of us that a hero must be handsome and possessed of great physical strength. Mr. Wilberforce was under five feet tall—certainly not an imposing stature even in his day. He was born in England in 1759. His family was of the landed nobility, so they were quite wealthy.

Besides being of unimpressive height, he also had several physical deformities. He was a hunchback, and his head leaned to one side. People thought him rather comical until they heard him speak. He had a powerful and compelling voice. Because he was a brilliant man, he also spoke eloquently. He ran for Parliament at the age of twenty-one, and because of his substantial oratorical gifts, was able to successfully campaign against older, more experienced men.

From this lofty forum, Mr. Wilberforce began to bring to the attention of his countrymen the horrors of slavery. At that time, few people were concerned. Slavery was an extremely profitable business, and its termination seemed virtually impossible, but William Wilberforce worked continually for its eradication even though for twenty years his fellow Parliamentarians voted down the legislation he proposed against this horrid economic practice. When finally the slave trade was abolished, he continued his battle for human rights for all men for another twenty-five years. Finally, when he was on his deathbed, he learned that seven hundred thousand British slaves had been set free! He inspired many others to stand up for the cause of freedom. A great university established for the children of former slaves in America bears his name in honor of his tireless efforts on the behalf of his Black brothers.

ROSA PARKS

It would be wonderful if the sad saga of slavery and all its lingering ramifications had ended then, but like so much of man's inhumanity against man, its hold was strong. A civil war had to be fought in the United States before this institution, conceived in hell, came to an end in North America; and even when it was officially over, the attitudes it engendered in the hearts and minds of people were a long time in dying. But throughout all the years of battling covert as well as overt prejudices rooted in the slave system, there have always been brave souls who stood against its pervasive impact over society.

One of those whose courage stands out as a beacon against the darkness is another unlikely warrior in the war for equality and justice. At one time, as recently as the mid-twentieth century, people of color in the southern United States were required to board the front of a bus, pay their fare, debark from the bus, go around to the back of the bus, and reenter from the rear, where they were allowed to be seated. If the front of the bus, which was reserved for "White" people became full, Black people in the back of the bus were required to give up their seats for the White passengers who would enter after their section became full!

We can scarcely imagine such a situation existing in the "land of the free and the home of the brave," but it did. Many White people realized it was wrong, but did nothing. Many Black people knew it was wrong, but felt helpless to do anything about it. Those who made an attempt to assert their right to be seated wherever they wished were beaten by the bus drivers or arrested for their efforts. No one knew for sure just how to solve the problem they all had to live with.

Then, on December 1, 1955, Rosa Parks joined the ranks of those who were willing to suffer any consequences that may come from refusing to comply with this prejudicial law. When required to give up her seat to a White passenger, she refused. The driver left the bus and returned with two policemen who arrested Mrs. Parks and took her to jail, where she was photographed and fingerprinted like a common criminal and scheduled her for trial on December 5. Mrs. Parks felt badly at the injustice of her treatment, but she knew she was doing right, and she prayed to God for the strength to endure the hardship of her situation.

She was taken to Montgomery, Alabama, where she was convicted of the charges against her. However, her lawyers took her case to the Supreme Court of the United States, and they ruled in her favor! Because of the courage of one obscure woman, many were emboldened to stand up against the lingering wrongs of slavery. Many people, both Black and White, have been set free from the bonds of prejudice because Rosa Parks was willing to be unjustly treated by a corrupt system so that that system could be corrected. For her brave stand as one flickering candle shining against the darkness, Mrs. Parks is called the "mother of the civil rights movement."

CORRIE TEN BOOM

At perhaps no other time in history was the need to stand against the madness of government gone awry more imperative than in Europe during the reign of terror imposed upon that continent and the world by Nazi Germany. During the awful days of World War II, good people in many parts of Europe stood by while horrible things were being done to their Jewish neighbors and friends. It was the time we now call the Holocaust, when the Nazis were unleashing a fury of hatred against God's ancient people.

Hatred is always ugly and destructive, but the intensity of the hatred the Nazis bore against the Jews grew to such magnitude that over six million innocent Jewish men, women, and children were killed by their oppressors during the course of the war. While most non-Jewish people stood by, justifying their indifference by rationalizing that there was nothing they could do anyway against such a massive war machine, a few realized that if they did not try to help, they could not count themselves guiltless of the innocent blood that was being spilled! They went about seeking to alleviate the suffering of their Jewish brothers, to stop the shedding of innocent blood, even at risk of mingling it with their own! One such family that joined the resistance movement to help the suffering Jews lived in Amsterdam, Holland.

The father owned a clock shop where he repaired broken timepieces. His daughters, Corrie and Betsy Ten Boom, lived with him and helped him at his trade. They decided to seal off a portion of their living quarters, which were in the same building as the clock shop, and use this secret part of their home as a place to hide Jews until arrangements could be made for their escape to a country that was not occupied by the Nazis. Many Jewish families, indeed, were helped to escape through the efforts of the Ten Boom family until the Nazis discovered the activity being conducted from the little clock shop!

Once arrested, Mr. Ten Boom, because he was elderly and quite frail, did not live very long. His daughter Betsy fared badly also, and after much hardship, died in a concentration camp.

Corrie Ten Boom, however, survived the concentration camp and lived to tell her story of God's faithfulness to her in the horrible days of prison. Miss Ten Boom lectured around the world on the importance of having the courage to fight against wrongs, the assurance that Jesus is always with those who suffer, and the importance of forgiving those whov'e wronged us.

After one of her lectures, a man approached her to say that he had been a prison guard at the concentration camp where her sister had died. Indeed, she recognized his face! She was almost overcome with revulsion at the sight of this man at whose hands she and her beloved Betsy had suffered. At that moment, she turned to Jesus for help. Of herself: she could not have granted the former prison guard the forgiveness for which he had asked her, but when she asked Jesus to help her, she was able to reach out and embrace in love and forgiveness a man who had once been her enemy but who was now her brother in Christ!

GEORGE WASHINGTON CARVER

Young people today may not face the same atrocities of World War II, but they are growing up in a world marked by war, violence, and deep division. Conflicts rage in Ukraine, the Middle East, and beyond, and even within our own communities and nation, hostility and hatred often seem to dominate. Many also struggle against the temptations of despair, addiction, loneliness, and the pull of online influences that diminish their worth and distract from what is good and true.

The battle against wrong—whether in the world around us or in our own hearts—still demands the same courage the Ten Boom family showed: the courage to stand for what is right, even when everyone else is silent or complicit. The same Jesus who sustained them through their darkest trials remains with us today. With Him as our commander-in-chief, we too can be victorious as we resist the forces that would harm the youth who are the heart and soul of our nation. It is His desire to give victory in every age, in every adversity, to every heart that belongs to Him.

Until the Industrial Revolution, life had gone on virtually the same as it had since the beginning of recorded history. Few people have had the insights to discover the secrets that unfolded in the twentieth century, and one of the most outstanding and gifted scientists whose contributions to the modern age have been phenomenal, was born a slave!

George Washington Carver supported himself while in college by doing laundry for wealthy people. He did an excellent job at laundry, even as he did at his studies at various institutions that were willing to accept Black students. He received his degree from Iowa State College, which had a fine agricultural program. After a brief stay on the faculty of Iowa State, he moved on to Alabama to join the staff of a small new school for Blacks, Tuskegee Institute.

Dr. Carver arrived at Tuskegee with just a box of beautiful stones he'd collected, a new microscope, which had been given to him by his friends at Iowa State, and his well-worn Bible. When he arrived, his laboratory was empty, but he and his students collected "junk" to use to build the things they'd need in their lab.

Within just three years, he'd taught his students how to make the poor soil productive and how to assure its continued productivity. He and his students traveled around Alabama demonstrating these techniques to poor farmers, and farming around the state improved!

When the boll weevil destroyed the cotton crop, Dr. Carver suggested planting peanuts. At the time, it was said that Dr. Carver, who was a deeply religious man, prayed a new prayer to God. He asked, "Lord, show me the secrets of Your universe." Dr. Carver said that God answered him and said, "Little man, the universe is too big for you! I'm going to teach you the secrets of the peanut!"

In his laboratory, George Washington Carver did discover the secrets of the peanut. He made 300 things from peanuts and 118 things from sweet potatoes! But fame and honor never diminished his sense of wonder at the world God had created, and he never lost his sense of humility in his pursuit of the knowledge God had hidden in ordinary things.

MOHANDAS GANDHI

Carver's story reminds us that virtue knows no boundaries — of race, status, or country. In another land and another culture, Mohandas Gandhi would also rise to show the world that goodness and courage can change history. Gandhi was as born on October 2, 1869, while his nation of India was still under British rule. His parents were of the Vaishya (merchant) caste of Hindus. At this time, the caste laws in India were very firmly entrenched. They forbade any significant interaction among people of differing castes.

This system of strict segregation was very harsh, but most of the people of India accepted it without question. Mohandas Gandhi believed all people should be considered equal and have equal access to opportunity. He also believed that the way a person behaved was more important than what he achieved, so he refused violence as a means of protest.

He spent twenty-one years in British-controlled South Africa, where he worked tirelessly for the rights of Indians who faced discrimination at the hands of their British rulers. When he returned to India, he carried his nonviolent war against discrimination back to his homeland with him.

His efforts resulted in success! India attained its independence from England in 1947. Perhaps if he had lived (he was assassinated by a ranking Indian in 1948), he could have helped his people overcome the prejudice they felt toward one another because of their differing castes.

The legacy he left of nonviolent protest was embraced a few decades later by the great American civil rights leader, The Reverend Dr. Martin Luther King Jr. Many people today enjoy freedom from prejudice and hatred in their hearts because of the example set by Mohandas Gandhi.

PRESIDENT ABRAHAM LINCOLN

By almost anyone's definition of strength, power—the ability to assert ourselves over those who are weaker—is included in the perception of the word. A bully is someone who doesn't believe in himself enough to share his space with another or allow them to have any space of their own. A truly big person is not intimidated by another individual making inroads into his space.

The sixteenth president of the United States of America, Abraham Lincoln, was a man possessed of great strength—physical and moral strength. He stood six foot four in a day when the average height for men was about five foot six. He towered over his diminutive wife, Mary Todd Lincoln, who was barely five feet tall.

Mrs. Lincoln, it is said, was given to outbursts of temper. At times, she would vent her frustrations by pursuing Mr. Lincoln around the house, hitting him with a broom! An observer to this spectacle refrained from laughing at the curious sight of this tiny woman unleashing her fury against a powerful man who could have easily subdued her. It is said that the observer inquired of Mr. Lincoln just why he allowed this affront to his dignity to occur. The president's response was, "The blows she delivers against me don't hurt me at all—and it seems to make her feel better!"

Because he knew his strength, Abe Lincoln did not need to demonstrate his strength! People who are possessed of true strength of body or strength of character do not feel threatened when opposed by someone weaker. They do not feel the necessity to assert their superiority by a display of their strength.

THE COSMOS AND THE CROSS

Lincoln's quiet strength was rooted in humility and awe of something greater than himself. Likewise, when American astronauts looked out at the vastness of space, they didn't claim the heavens as their own but instead honored the One who made them. During the Cold War that occurred in the mid to late twentieth century, the competition between the old Soviet Union and the United States of America was quite intense. This competitive attitude between the two superpowers was nowhere more evident than in the space race.

The Soviet Union took the lead early in the race when, in 1957, they launched the first manmade satellite to ever orbit the earth. The United States was stunned, not just by this accomplishment, but also by the harsh reality of its own unpreparedness to compete! The nation realized it would be left in the dust of Soviet space technology if space were not given top priority! It was.

Through the subsequent years, many more satellites and space probes, manned and unmanned, were launched by both sides. The world watched in awe as one nation, then the other took the lead with some new technological marvel, unprecedented in the annals of human accomplishment.

In the midst of all this modern electronic and computer wizardry that fed the space programs of both nations, there still existed one age old question, "Who is God, and where does He exist?" Astronauts and cosmonauts were darting back and forth in space. Some Soviet cosmonauts were reported to have been lost in secret missions. American astronauts came perilously close to death in the Apollo 13 mission, even as the world watched and prayed.

In an effort to promote their atheistic worldview, Soviet propagandists circulated the claim that a cosmonaut had returned from space saying, "I have been to space, I have searched for God in heaven, and He is not here." By contrast, American astronauts sometimes read scripture verses from their "pulpit" in space, and many were touched so deeply with awe by their experience in "the second heaven," as the Bible refers to the realm above our atmosphere, that they later became preachers or evangelists!

The contrast is striking and reflective of a similar drama played out on a hillside called Golgotha in the city of Jerusalem two thousand years ago. Three men, all Hebrew by birth, were convicted by the Roman occupational government and sentenced to a horrid death they'd contrived called crucifixion. In the center hung Jesus Christ, who purported Himself to be the Son of God, coming from heaven on His Father's mission—to bear upon His own sinless body the punishment for all the sins of all the people who had ever or would ever live on earth. The flesh of His back had been shredded by the forty lashes save one He'd received from the notorious Roman cat-o'-nine-tails, a whip with nine lashes instead of one. His face was encrusted with blood from having the hair of His beard pulled from his face. His brow was streaked with blood that flowed from the crown of thorns that had been pressed into His scalp. His wrists and feet were pierced with large spikes that had been driven into His flesh to secure Him to the instrument of torture upon which He had been hung.

On either side of the cross of Jesus hung two criminals who shared his fate that day. One was convicted of theft, the other of murder and insurrection. One railed at Jesus, "You saved others; if You're who You claim to be, save Yourself from this horror, and save us too!"

The other criminal said to the one who challenged Jesus, "You and I deserve to be here, but this just man does not!" In the moment when he defended the God-Man hanging between them, the second criminal's attitude changed. As he defended Christ's innocence, he began to see His holiness! He turned to Jesus and said to Him, "Jesus, remember me when you come into your kingdom."

Jesus promised him at that moment, "Today you will be with me in Paradise" (Luke 23:39–43, NRSV).

What made one criminal hanging on a cross mock his fellow-sufferer, while another bowed his heart before Jesus? All either saw was another dying man enduring the pain and humiliation of crucifixion, but while one saw merely a condemned man expiring cruelly on a cross, the other saw his Savior.

What made the Soviets Union to brazenly assert that God could not possibly exist in heaven? What caused the American astronauts to be humbled before the majesty of God that they saw revealed in their brief sojourn in the second heaven?

What makes the difference for each of them is the same thing that makes the difference for each of us in our perceptions of life's choices. Do we believe that God loves us and delights in us when we choose to allow our life's decisions to be directed by virtue? Or do we see ourselves as free moral agents, unbounded by restraints of any sort?

Faith in God is the heart of virtue. Just as life ceases when the heart stops, so does true virtue cease when faith stops. To restore goodness of character, moral excellence, right thinking and right action, which are part of what virtue encompasses, to a society woefully lacking in them, we need a spiritual revival that will open our hearts to God again! He has promised that He will be found by those who seek Him, and He will dwell in the hearts of those who love Him. With Christ in residence, the reader's pulse will pound with faith, and the reader's life will be alive with virtue!

ABOUT THE AUTHOR

Sandra L. DiNello was born in 1944 in New Brighton, Pennsylvania, where she cultivated a lifelong love of learning and literature. She earned a scholarship to Geneva College, graduating with a degree in English, and later married Philip L. DiNello, Jr., a civil engineer with the U.S. Army Corps of Engineers. Together, they raised two children, Stephen and Joelle, and Sandra now delights in being grandmother to five grandchildren: Hannah, Naomi, Anna, Calah, and Micah.

Sandra served as an elementary and middle school educator for over three decades, beginning in the 1960s and retiring in the early 2000s. Throughout those years, hundreds of students passed through her classrooms, where they were not only taught but nurtured with compassion, humor, and a deep sense of calling. Among her most memorable contributions was the extraordinarily popular geography club, where students didn't just memorize countries — they encountered the world through cultural artifacts, stories, traditional cuisine, dress, and guest speakers from around the globe. These immersive experiences opened young hearts to the beauty and dignity of all people and inspired a lasting love for the world beyond their own borders.

From 1980 to 1985, Sandra and her family lived in Saudi Arabia, where Philip was stationed. There, she had the unique opportunity to build friendships with people from many nations and cultures. Her passion for virtue — as a lived, cross-cultural reality — deepened. Her life has reflected the beauty of the cardinal virtues: prudence, justice, fortitude, and temperance, all rooted in the theological virtues of faith, hope, and love.

Since the mid-1980s, she has lived in Winchester, Virginia, where she has faithfully served her church community. She is an extraordinary cook who delights friends, missionaries, and especially family with warm hospitality and unforgettable meals — none more beloved than her world-famous Sunday gnocchi and meatballs.

In all things, Sandra seeks to reflect Christ's love into the world — through her words, her table, and her life.

KRISTEN MILLER'S BIOGRAPHY

Kristen Miller serves as Connections & Women's Pastor at Abundant Life Church, located in Stephens City/Winchester, Virginia. She has ministered alongside her husband, Lead Pastor John Miller, at Abundant Life since 2004, contributing to the church's growth into a vibrant, multi-site congregation.

In her role, Kristen oversees the church's Women's Ministry and the Connections ministry – helping newcomers integrate into the community, guiding growth tracks, and equipping women to exercise their gifts in faith and service.

Kristen and John are parents to three children: two married daughters and a son, Josiah; and two grandchildren.

Her leadership is marked by warmth, accessibility, and a deep commitment to helping people connect with Jesus and each other.

As the author of the foreword for *Always Do What's Good: A Small History of Virtue*, Kristen brings a heart for character formation, cross-generational faith, and the transformation of everyday life by virtue and grace. Her participation underscores the book's aim to nurture young hearts in courage, integrity and faith.

www.ingramcontent.com/pod-product-compliance
Lightning Source LLC
Chambersburg PA
CBHW041403090426

42743CB00006B/137